Do I really look like that?

Surely I'm not getting fat.

Last week I was really good,
I only ate just what I should.

Exercise? I always do!
You only have to see my shoe.

I ran to the shops
and bussed it back.

Willpower is one thing I don't lack.

Chocolate is good for you.

That creamy bun would never do.

6

It's much too cold for salad and veg.
That would push me over the edge.

7

I said no to chips and mash,
and settled for the corned beef hash,

followed by apple crumble
and cream.
To touch the ice cream
I wouldn't dream!

9

The fourteen dress
I bought for a song...
The label in the back
just has to be wrong.

This week I'll be really good.

That mirror will go, I don't like the wood.

11

About the Author

I was born and grew up in Manchester and I am proud of our city.
I am a 66 year old grandmother with 7 grandchildren,
2 boys and 5 girls.
I read with my grandchildren
and get lots of pleasure sharing my books with them.

I love reading and hope you will too.
It helps me to picture other people and their lives.
Reading a book can help me forget my problems
and become part of another world for a time.

I am a member of a writing group.
I write about everyday things and ordinary people.
I also paint in watercolour and oil
and I feel my poems are painting with words.

I wrote this poem at a slimming class
because I am an expert at losing weight and diets.
It is meant to be fun and so I gave it in as a story
hoping someone else would read it, laugh and enjoy it.

If you enjoy it, why don't you try
to write about some time in your life
that has made you laugh.
Since writing my poem I am now writing more.
It has given me the confidence to try new things.

Jean Garvey

Dedication

This book is dedicated to Olive Cordell,
Chair of Gatehouse for 12 years.

Olive was:

- a great teacher who believed in learning for all
- a woman who inspired people and made them laugh
- a lover of good food, wine and fun
- a hater of diets
- a woman with style and presence
- my mum and my best friend.

She died the day before her 63rd birthday on 20th August 2002.
A piece of me died with her that day.

She would have liked this book –

I am sorry she can't read it,
but I hope you enjoy it and that it makes you laugh.

Jane Cordell

Gatehouse Books

Gatehouse is a unique publisher

Our writers are adults who are developing their basic
reading and writing skills. Their ideas and experiences
make fascinating material for any reader, but are
particularly relevant for adults working on their reading and
writing skills. The writing strikes a chord - a shared
experience of struggling against many odds.

The format of our books is clear and uncluttered. The
language is familiar and the text is often line-broken, so
that each line ends at a natural pause.

Gatehouse books are both popular and respected within
Adult Basic Education throughout the English speaking
world. They are also a valuable resource within secondary
schools, Social Services and within the Prison Education
Service and Probation Services.

Booklist available

Gatehouse Books
Hulme Adult Education Centre
Stretford Road
Manchester
M15 5FQ
Tel: 0161 226 7152
Fax: 0161 868 0351
E-mail: office@gatehousebooks.org.uk
Website: www.gatehousebooks.org.uk